This book is intended for information and inspiration only. It does not offer medical, psychological, legal or financial advice. Readers assume full responsibility for their decisions and actions.

Published by The WOW Book Co.
Austin, Texas

ISBN: 978-1-967973-81-1
Title: Reinvention Bot
Subtitle: A ChatGPT-Powered Guide to Resetting Your Life and Becoming Who You Were Meant to Be
Author: Sugar Gay Isber McMillan

Printed in the United States of America.
For more information or permissions, contact: GayIsber@gmail.com

REINVENTION
BOT
SUGAR GAY ISBER MCMILLAN

Introduction: The Life You Build From Here

There comes a moment in every life when the old version of you stops fitting. You feel it in the quiet places inside yourself. Something shifts. Something stirs. Something whispers, *I'm different now.*

That whisper is not dramatic. It is not a crisis. It is not a breakdown. It is the beginning of reinvention.

Reinvention does not require burning your life down or becoming someone unrecognizable. It begins with one honest decision:
I am ready to change.

Most people think reinvention demands huge moves. New cities. New careers. New versions of themselves that feel impossible to reach. But real reinvention is quieter and more human. It starts with clarity. With truth. With the willingness to stop carrying the stories, habits and identities that no longer feel like you.

This book gives you a clear, simple map for that work.
You will learn how to build your next era with daily actions, bold choices and thoughtful conversations with your Reinvention Bot, a tool that helps you think clearly and imagine yourself forward.

Through each chapter, you will be invited to:

- release the patterns that kept you small
- rewrite your inner story
- choose habits and spaces that support your new identity
- build confidence through small, steady acts of courage
- step toward the future you want with clarity and intention

Reinvention belongs to everyone.
To people starting over after years of living for others.
To people becoming honest about who they are.
To people retiring and wondering what comes next.
To people rebuilding after loss or burnout.
To people waking up and realizing they want more than they have allowed themselves to want.

No matter your age or stage, you can choose a new beginning. You can choose the version of yourself you were meant to be. You can choose to live a life that feels true and grounded.

This is the work of becoming.
Quiet. Steady. Strong.

Turn the page.
Your next era begins
here and now.

PART ONE: RELEASE

Chapter 1. Cut the Chaos

Reinvention begins with subtraction. Before you build a new version of yourself, you clear out the forces that drain clarity, energy, and direction. Most people try to change their life while still carrying the people, habits, and emotional clutter that created their old reality. That never works.

There is almost always one person who brings confusion, tension, drama, or distraction into your world. You already know who it is. Reinvention requires removing that influence, not because you're cruel or cold, but because you're done negotiating with chaos.

This is not a confrontation. This is an act of choosing yourself.

You don't need a speech. You don't need a debate. You don't need to justify your decision, and you don't need permission to draw a boundary. You simply stop participating in the dynamic that keeps you small. Reinvention begins in the moment you say, "No more."

Your Action Step

Send one clear message.

Not emotional.
Not long.
Not open-ended.

A message that closes the loop without creating new noise.

Something like:

"I'm stepping into a new phase of my life and won't be available for this dynamic anymore. I wish you well."

That's it.
You won't argue.
You won't negotiate.
You won't explain.
Your future does not need defending.

How ChatGPT Helps

If you struggle to word it cleanly, ask:

"Help me write a concise, respectful message to distance myself from someone whose energy is no longer aligned with the life I'm building. Keep it calm and final."

You'll receive a clear, neutral boundary you can use as-is or adjust. The tool doesn't judge, react, or add emotion. It simply helps you craft closure.

Why This Matters

When you remove the primary source of chaos, everything else sharpens:

- your thinking
- your routine
- your goals
- your confidence
- your identity

There is no reinvention without release.
And this first release teaches your mind a new pattern:
You are allowed to remove what no longer supports the person you're becoming.

This is Step One.
The rebuilding begins here.

Chapter 2. Retire the Old Stories

Reinvention isn't blocked by circumstances. It's blocked by the stories you repeat about your circumstances.

Everyone carries a set of narratives they've told for years. These stories feel true because they've been rehearsed, not because they reflect your current reality. The brain loves familiar patterns, even when the pattern hurts.

The past only has power when you retell it.

The moment you stop giving airtime to the problems, betrayals, disappointments and limitations you've rehearsed, the identity built around them dissolves. You can't step into a new chapter while quoting the old one.

This isn't denial.
It's direction.

You acknowledge what happened, then you choose not to anchor your identity to it anymore.

Your Action Step

Catch yourself the next time you start telling an old emotional script. You'll recognize it by its tone:

- tired
- repetitive
- familiar
- identity-shaping
- past-tense heavy
- problem-anchored

Pause and say, quietly or aloud:

"That story is retired."

Replacing a narrative doesn't require therapy, closure or deep analysis. It requires repetition of a new identity, not repetition of an old wound.

How ChatGPT Helps

Ask:

"Rewrite this story from a point of strength. Show me what it looks like when I take the lesson and leave the pain."

Paste the old narrative if you want.
Or summarize it in a few lines.

You'll receive a version rooted in clarity, dignity and forward motion.
Something your mind can rehearse instead of the old loop.

You can also ask:

"Help me create a one-sentence replacement for this limiting story."

You'll get a simple phrase to use like a reset switch.

Why This Matters

Your identity is built on the stories you repeat, not the events themselves. When you retire the tired narrative, you shift from reacting to the past to authoring the future.

Reinvention requires this mental break.
It teaches you that you are not the narrator of an old chapter.
You are the architect of a new one.

When the story changes, the future opens.

Chapter 3. Clean the Closet, Clean the Identity

The fastest way to change how you see yourself is to change what you reach for every morning.

Clothes carry identity.
You bought them during a specific worldview, a specific season of life, a specific version of yourself. When that version no longer fits, the clothing starts to feel heavy, outdated or disconnected.

Reinvention requires clearing out the artifacts of your old identity.

Not because they are bad.
Because they are anchored to a self you are outgrowing.

If you want your future to feel different, your daily cues must change. A closet full of old-self clothing quietly reinforces the past every time you open the door.

This is not a decluttering task.
It is an identity reset.

Your Action Step

Remove every item that belongs to an older version of you.

No half-keeping.
No "just in case."
No nostalgia masquerading as utility.

If an item carries the energy of:

- limitation
- insecurity
- stagnation
- regret

- people you no longer want in your orbit
- or a chapter that is closed

…it goes.

You are clearing space for the next version of you to exist physically, not just mentally.

How ChatGPT Helps

Ask:

"Help me define the visual style of the identity I'm stepping into. Describe the colors, textures, silhouettes and overall feeling of this future version of me."

You'll receive a style brief that feels aligned and intentional.
This gives you a filter:

If it doesn't fit the brief, it doesn't stay.

You can also ask:

"Help me create a simple clothing philosophy for my next chapter."

This becomes a guide you can use for future purchases.

Why This Matters

Every object in your environment either reinforces who you were or supports who you're becoming. Clothing holds more emotional data than people realize.

This step teaches your brain a new rule:
The old life no longer lives here.

When you open a closet full of things that match your future identity, reinvention stops being an idea and becomes a daily experience.

Chapter 4. Delete the Soundtrack of Your Old Life

Music is memory.
Songs are emotional anchors.
Playlists carry entire identities inside them.

You may not realize it, but the music you listen to most often is tied directly to who you were when you added those songs. The moods, relationships, jobs, hopes, hurts and habits of that era still live inside those tracks.

When you're reinventing yourself, the soundtrack of your past can quietly keep you tied to it.

Your brain is associative.
If the music stays the same, the emotional wiring stays the same.

Reinvention requires disrupting the emotional cues that pull you back into old patterns. A fresh identity needs a fresh sound.

This isn't about taste.
It's about direction.

Your Action Step

Delete every playlist that feels like a soundtrack to your old life.

Not the songs that still genuinely move you — those stay.
But the playlists that represent:

- heartbreak
- stagnation
- ruts
- past relationships

- old versions of confidence
- seasons you've outgrown
- periods of chaos
- emotional loops you've already healed

Those playlists keep your nervous system wired to history.
Letting them go frees up emotional bandwidth for the future.

How ChatGPT Helps

Ask:

"Create a playlist theme or concept for the identity I'm stepping into. Focus on the emotional tone, not specific songs."

You'll rcceive a vibe description:
Upward. Clean. Strong. Clear. Focused. Expansive.

Once you have the tone, you can build a playlist that supports who you are becoming, not who you once were.

You can also ask:

"Give me a list of words or phrases that describe the emotional energy of my next chapter."

Use those words to guide your song choices.

Why This Matters

Your brain loves repetition.
If you feed it the music of the past, it will replay the emotions of the past.

Reinvention is not just cognitive.
It is sensory.

When the soundtrack changes, your inner state changes.
When your inner state changes, your identity follows.

This is the quiet power of Release.
Removing the emotional cues of your old life creates space for something new to take root.

Chapter 5. Unfollow the Past

Your digital world shapes your identity just as much as your physical world. Every account you follow, every feed you consume and every person you watch—even silently—pulls you toward a particular emotional and mental state.

Most people never notice the effect.

You see someone's posts enough times and their worldview becomes part of yours. You absorb their tone, their values, their anxieties, their ambitions, their drama. Digital proximity becomes emotional proximity.

Reinvention requires curating the voices you allow into your mind.

Just like you cleared your closet, you now clear your feed.
You remove the accounts tied to old identities, old relationships, old insecurities and old habits. You unfollow anyone who makes your mind feel cluttered, heavy, smaller or stagnant.

This isn't personal.
It's directional.

You're choosing what gets space in the next era of your life.

Your Action Step

Unfollow every account that no longer aligns with:

- the direction you're going
- the identity you're building
- the values you want to reinforce
- the energy you want in your world
- the emotional tone you want daily

- the habits you're cultivating
- the future version of yourself you're stepping into

You're not judging these people.
You're adjusting your inputs.

When you change the content you consume, you change the content of your thoughts.

How ChatGPT Helps

Ask:

"Help me describe the identity I'm building. List the qualities, habits and mindsets that define the next version of me."

Once you have that profile, use it as your filter.
If an account doesn't match that direction, it's not coming with you.

You can also ask:

"Help me create a guideline for the kind of content that supports my next chapter."

You'll get a clear, personalized criteria list.

Why This Matters

Your feed is a mirror.
If it reflects the past, you stay in the past.
If it reflects the future, you grow toward it.

This chapter marks the final digital release.
Once you clean your inputs, your identity becomes easier to shape.

You cannot build a new life on the architecture of an old algorithm.
Reinvention begins with intentional attention.

Chapter 6. Leave the Old Patterns with Fire

Reinvention requires a moment of symbolic closure.
A line drawn in the sand.
A declaration that the version of you who tolerated the old patterns is gone.

Most people try to change quietly. They attempt a soft shift, hoping their life will slowly adjust itself. But reinvention accelerates when there is a moment of decision—one your brain understands as final.

You need a ritual that marks the end of your former limits.

The simplest and most powerful ritual is this:
Write down the beliefs, habits and behaviors you're done carrying, then release them through fire.

Not because fire is mystical.
Because your brain understands the symbolism of destruction and completion.

When you burn something, you tell your mind:
This will not follow me into my next chapter.

This ritual works because it engages your senses.
You see the old identity dissolve.
You hear the crackle of release.
You feel the warmth of finality.
Your nervous system understands: "We're done here."

Your Action Step

Take a sheet of paper and write down:

- the habits that keep you stuck
- the beliefs that shrink your confidence

- the patterns you repeat out of fear
- the behaviors you inherited but never chose
- the emotional loops that drain you
- the excuses that held you in place
- the versions of you that no longer belong

Then take that list outside.
Light it safely.
Watch it burn.

Say quietly (or aloud):

"I release these patterns. They are not part of my future."

You don't need a ceremony.
You need a moment.

How ChatGPT Helps

Ask:

"Help me identify the beliefs, habits or behaviors that are holding me back from becoming the person I want to be."

You'll get a list of patterns—clean, objective, and free of judgment. This helps clarify what goes on the paper.

You can also ask:

"Help me write a short release statement that marks the end of my old identity and the beginning of a new one."

Use that statement before or after the ritual.

Why This Matters

Reinvention isn't only mental.
It requires a physical break in the pattern.

When you burn the old list, your brain stops treating those patterns as part of your identity. The ritual signals the end of compliance with your old self.

Release is complete. The next chapter begins.

PART TWO: REBUILD

Chapter 7. Spend a Day Meeting Your Next-Era Self

Reinvention doesn't start with goals.
It starts with identity.

You cannot build a new life with the mindset that shaped the old one. Before you redesign your habits, your space, your routines or your relationships, you need a clear understanding of the person you are becoming.

Most people try to reinvent their life without upgrading the identity behind it.
The result is frustration, self-sabotage or slipping back into old patterns.

Your next era begins the moment you decide who you are now becoming.

This version of you already exists as a possibility. You are not imagining them. You are recognizing the blueprint that has been waiting beneath the surface.

Your job is to meet them clearly.

Your Action Step

Set aside one uninterrupted day—or a few quiet hours—to define your next-era self.
Ask questions like:

- How does this version of me think?
- What do they consider important?
- What do they no longer tolerate?
- How do they speak to themselves?
- What does their environment look like?
- What do they wear?
- What habits feel natural to them?
- What emotions shape their days?
- What are they building?
- What are they restoring?
- What do they release without guilt?
- What would they say no to immediately?
- What would they say yes to without overthinking?

Write freely.
No judgment.
This is not about the life you "should" want or the identity you think others expect.
This is about the person you are becoming.

How ChatGPT Helps

Ask:

"Help me write a detailed identity profile for the version of myself I am becoming. Include mindset, habits, values, tone, behaviors, and how they approach challenges."

You will receive a clear identity map—something most people never create in their entire lives.
This map becomes the reference point for every decision you make going forward.

You can also ask:

"What would be the daily habits of someone with this identity?"

And:

"What would this version of me eliminate from their life immediately?"

ChatGPT helps you see blind spots, anchors, and opportunities you might not recognize alone.

Why This Matters

Identity drives behavior.
Behavior drives outcomes.
Outcomes create your lived reality.

When your identity shifts, everything else becomes easier:

- discipline
- boundaries
- habits
- decisions
- confidence
- direction

You stop trying to force yourself into change and start acting from the future instead of the past.
This is the moment reinvention becomes natural.

Meet your next-era self.
They are waiting for you.

Chapter 8. Journal From Your Future Self Daily

There is a version of you who already solved the problems you're facing now.
They've made the decisions you are still hesitating over.
They've stepped into the confidence you're learning to claim.
They've become the person you're building toward.

Reinvention becomes real when you stop trying to transform from the past and begin speaking from the future.

Most people journal from their present struggles.
They write about what they're afraid of, what they regret, what isn't working, and what they wish they could change.
But that kind of journaling quietly reinforces the old identity. It documents the self you're trying to leave behind.

Future-self journaling does the opposite.
It builds the path forward.

It allows you to think from the identity you are becoming, not the one you've been repeating.

The Quiet Power of Letters From Tomorrow

If you've ever received a letter that changed your life, you know the impact of words coming from a place you haven't yet reached.

Future-self journaling works the same way.
It gives you guidance from someone who already knows the way.

Here is what happens when you journal from your future:

- you bypass fear
- you stop negotiating with doubt
- you speak with clarity instead of confusion
- you see solutions you missed the day before
- you begin to act like the person you're becoming

It feels like borrowing wisdom from your own potential.

A Story From Real Life

There was a man who wanted to reinvent his life after losing his job of twenty years. He felt directionless, angry at himself, and convinced he didn't have the skills to start over. A friend told him to try writing a single paragraph each morning as if it came from the version of himself who had already rebuilt his career.

For the first few days, he resisted.
It felt strange.
Forced.
Unrealistic.

But by the end of the first week, the letters changed.
His future self began writing with authority:

"You already know what to do. You've survived worse. You're not starting at zero — you're starting with experience. You're creative. You adapt. Trust me. Keep going."

Within a month, he began acting differently.
Within three months, he had created a consulting service in the same field he once worked for someone else.
Within a year, he was fully self-employed — something he never thought possible.

He said later, "I didn't become someone new. I finally listened to the version of me who wasn't afraid."

That is the power of writing from the future.

Your Action Step

Each morning, open a notebook and write as if the next-era version of you is sending a message back through time.

Write from the perspective of someone who:

- already achieved what you're working toward
- already healed what you're currently processing
- already made the difficult decisions
- already stood up for themselves
- already learned discipline, clarity and courage
- already changed their environment
- already stepped into a bigger life

Write as if you are closing the gap between where you are and where you're going — because you are.

If you don't know what to write, begin with:

"I want you to know…"
or
"Here's what you're ready for…"
or
"You're overthinking this because…"
or
"Stop avoiding what you already know…"
or
"This is the day you finally…"

Let the tone be direct.
Future You doesn't waste time.
They speak clearly because they already walked the road you're just starting.

How ChatGPT Helps

Ask:

"Write a daily letter to me from the version of myself who has already achieved the identity and life I'm building. Make it strong, encouraging and specific."

You can request:

- monthly versions
- career-focused versions
- relationship-focused versions
- financial versions
- confidence-building versions
- discipline-building versions
- health-focused versions

Every letter becomes a micro-adjustment to your identity.

Another powerful prompt:

"What does my future self want me to stop doing immediately?"

Or:

"What mindset shift would the future version of me insist on today?"

ChatGPT becomes the bridge between your current self and your next-era self.

Why This Matters

Most people never rise above the level of the story they tell themselves before breakfast.
But when you begin the day with guidance from your future, your entire orientation changes.

Future-self journaling trains you to:

- think ahead
- expect growth
- choose strength
- live in possibility
- speak from clarity
- steer your day intentionally

It is not about predicting the future.
It is about pulling your identity forward, one page at a time.

Write the letters.
Let the future speak.
Let the new identity take shape at the speed of ink.

Chapter 9. Install a Signature Goal

Reinvention thrives on direction.
It doesn't need ten goals.
It needs one.

A single, specific, identity-shaping goal will pull you out of your old patterns faster than any amount of motivation, journaling or self-reflection. It becomes a lighthouse. A point of orientation. The first anchor of your future.

Without a signature goal, reinvention stays theoretical.
With one, it becomes physical.

Why One Goal Matters

Human beings work best with a central focus.
One clear direction begins to reorganize everything: your habits, your discipline, your schedule, your environment, your energy.

You can feel it.

This isn't about productivity.
It's about identity.

When you choose a goal that requires a new version of you, your old patterns can't survive. They don't fit the structure anymore.

A Story From the Edge of Retirement

A man named Paul retired at sixty-two after forty years in logistics. He told everyone that he was excited to rest, but privately he felt unmoored. For months he drifted through his days. He slept in. Watched TV. Ran errands that didn't matter. His energy dropped. His confidence slipped. His world felt smaller every week.

One afternoon, while sorting old boxes in his garage, he found a dusty notebook filled with sketches from his twenties. Drawings of furniture he once dreamed of building. A life he never pursued because "adulthood got in the way."

That night he wrote one sentence:

"My signature goal is to build one piece of furniture worthy of passing down."

Small.
Clear.
Specific.

It changed everything.

He signed up for a woodworking class.
He blocked two mornings a week for shop time.
He started researching hardwoods.
He woke up earlier.
He took himself seriously again.

By the end of nine months, he completed a custom walnut table that his daughter now treasures.

He didn't reinvent his whole life.
He reinvented one direction of it — and the rest followed.

This is the power of a signature goal.
It gives purpose to the space that opens after an old identity ends.

Your Signature Goal

Your signature goal is not a resolution.
It is not a bucket-list item.
It is not about checking something off.

A signature goal is a **directional identity tool**.

It has three qualities:

1. It calls you forward.
2. It requires growth.
3. It introduces you to the next version of yourself.

A good signature goal is something that makes you straighten your posture a little. Something that adds a spark to your day. Something that wouldn't quite make sense for the old version of you, but fits the person you're becoming.

Here are examples:

- write the book you've been avoiding
- start a small business or side project
- learn a skill that opens new work possibilities
- volunteer in a way that rebuilds your sense of purpose
- train for something you've never tried before
- create art that represents a new era of your life
- build a healthier routine
- speak a new language
- make something with your hands
- mentor someone who needs your experience
- create a second-act career after retirement

The goal is not the point.
The identity it creates is.

Your Action Step

Choose one signature goal that meets these criteria:

- It excites you
- It intimidates you
- It demands consistency
- It would impress your future self
- It would surprise your past self

Write it clearly and commit to it.

Not with pressure.
With intention.

Then ask yourself:

"What habits does someone with this goal practice?"
"What do they no longer waste time on?"
"What choices feel obvious to this version of me?"

Let the answers guide your behavior.

How ChatGPT Helps

Ask:

"Help me define a signature goal for the next era of my life. I want something that stretches my identity and gives me direction."

You can also request:

"Break this goal into simple milestones that keep me consistent."
"What habits would support someone pursuing this goal?"
"What obstacles should I expect and how do I plan for them?"

You will get a road map that transforms intention into momentum.

If you're retiring or entering a second act, ask:

"Give me five identity-expanding signature goals for someone transitioning into retirement who wants purpose, structure and renewal."

Reinvention thrives on clarity.
Your signature goal provides it.

Why This Matters

When life shifts — retirement, a career change, a loss, an unexpected ending — the absence of direction can feel like falling.

A signature goal gives you gravity again.
It pulls you into your next era with focus instead of fear.

Reinvention isn't powered by willpower.
It's powered by alignment.

One good goal can change the entire architecture of your days.
Let it reshape you.

Chapter 10. Surround Yourself with Beauty

Reinvention isn't only about habits or mindset. It's also about environment.
Where you live, sit, work, rest, and think tells your nervous system who you are. Your surroundings either anchor you to the past or call you into the future.

Beauty is not decoration.
Beauty is information.
It signals that life can be meaningful, intentional, orderly, hopeful and spacious.

When your environment feels heavy, cluttered or neglected, your identity reflects that.
But when your environment feels cared for, elevated or inspiring, your identity expands to match it.

The Subtle Power of What You See Every Day

There's a reason hotels feel relaxing and bookstores feel creative and museums feel expansive. Spaces carry energy. They communicate possibility. They shape behavior without a word.

Your home does this too.
Every room quietly influences how you think.

Reinvention becomes easier when your space begins sending messages that say:

"You're allowed to grow."
"You're allowed to evolve."
"You're allowed to expect more."
"You're allowed to create something better."

Beauty makes change feel natural.

A Story About a Chair and a Window

There was a woman named Elena who felt stuck after a divorce. Her house felt like a museum of the past. Every room carried memories she wasn't ready to revisit, so she avoided her home by staying out late and filling her days with noise.

One morning she walked past a thrift store and saw a weathered but elegant armchair in the window. She didn't need it. She didn't even know where she would put it. But something in her paused — not at the chair, but at the idea that she could choose something beautiful just for herself.

She bought it.

She placed it near a window she had ignored for years. She added a lamp. A small table. A plant she promised herself she would keep alive. She sat in that chair every morning with her coffee. Just ten minutes. No phone. No pressure.

Within a month, the room felt different.
Within three months, she felt different.

Buying the chair didn't fix her life.
But it changed the direction of her days.

Sometimes reinvention begins with one small space that feels like the future, not the past.

Your Action Step

Look at the spaces you inhabit most:

- the kitchen
- the bedroom

- your desk
- your living room
- the bathroom mirror
- your nightstand
- your car

Ask one question:
"Does this space reflect who I'm becoming or who I used to be?"

If the answer leans toward the past, make a simple upgrade:

- add a plant
- clear a surface
- replace one object
- introduce real light or softer light
- remove anything that feels emotionally heavy
- bring in something that feels joyful, modern or alive
- frame something that inspires you
- rearrange furniture to change the energy flow
- add color
- add texture
- remove clutter that whispers the old story

Reinvention doesn't have to be expensive.
It has to be symbolic.

How ChatGPT Helps

Ask:

"Help me create a beauty blueprint for my living space that matches the identity I'm stepping into."

Or:

"Give me five small ways to elevate my environment without spending much money."

Or:

"What is one thing I can change in my space today that will make me feel more grounded in my next chapter?"

Your tool can also generate:

- color palettes
- minimalist reset plans
- micro-decluttering lists
- mood-setting suggestions
- daily environmental rituals

Why This Matters

Your environment is the stage where your identity performs.
If the stage stays the same, the performance rarely changes.

When you surround yourself with beauty — even small moments of it — you remind your mind that life can still surprise you, support you, elevate you, and hold you.

Beauty whispers, "There is more for you."
And you begin to believe it.

Chapter 11. Change Your Environment

When you stay in the same surroundings long enough, the space begins to script your behavior. You walk the same paths, think the same thoughts, repeat the same routines, and unconsciously replay the same emotional patterns. Reinvention requires interrupting this loop.

Changing your environment isn't about running away.
It's about creating new cues that support your next identity.

Even small environmental shifts can pull your mind into a fresh state.
Movement creates momentum.

Why Environment Shapes Identity

Your brain is constantly scanning for familiarity.
When it sees the same rooms, the same lighting, the same furniture, the same desk, the same corner of the sofa — it predicts what will happen next. It keeps you in yesterday's habits.

But when the environment changes, even in subtle ways, your brain wakes up. It becomes more alert, more curious, more flexible. This is where reinvention thrives.

You're not trying to become someone new inside the exact same frame.
You're widening the frame so new behavior fits more naturally.

A Story About a Man Who Rearranged His Entire Life by Moving a Chair

Years ago, a software engineer named Marcus fell into a rut after losing a promotion to someone ten years younger. He didn't want to change jobs, but he couldn't shake the feeling that he had become invisible in his own career.

One Sunday morning he moved a chair in his office so it faced a window instead of a wall. That was it. One chair. But something shifted.

Sitting in that new spot gave him fresh perspective. He began sketching ideas he had put off for years. Within a few weeks he reorganized the entire room. He added softer lighting. Placed a plant by the window. Cleared out old binders from a past job. Removed the visual reminders of a version of himself he no longer wanted to be.

Three months later he submitted a proposal for a new internal program. Six months later he was leading it.

He said, "I didn't change my life. I changed where I was sitting." Sometimes the smallest environmental shift unlocks the largest internal one.

Your Action Step

Change your environment this week. Not later. Not when you have time. Now.

Here are simple shifts with disproportionate impact:

- rearrange a room
- replace one tired object with something meaningful
- swap harsh lighting for warm light
- clear one cluttered surface completely
- create a dedicated corner for reading, thinking or planning
- change the scent of a room
- spend a morning working somewhere new

- take a walk in a different neighborhood
- visit a library, museum or public space you've never seen
- eat a meal on your back porch instead of in front of a screen

Even a one-time change can interrupt the psychological pattern that keeps you stuck in yesterday's identity.

If you're entering retirement or a new life phase, environmental change becomes even more valuable. When the structure of your days disappears, your surroundings must provide direction. Movement replaces stagnation. Novelty replaces drift.

How ChatGPT Helps

Ask:

"Give me five simple environmental changes I can make this week to feel more aligned with the identity I'm building."

Or:

"Help me redesign one corner of my home so it feels like the next chapter of my life."

Or:

"Suggest small, low-cost ways to change the energy of my living space."

You can also ask:

"What is one new place I can visit this week to expand my mind and break out of routine?"

Your tool becomes a source of fresh ideas, structure and momentum.

Why This Matters

Environment shapes mood.
Mood shapes behavior.
Behavior shapes identity.

When you change your environment, you send a message to your nervous system:

"We're not repeating the past anymore."

This is not about aesthetics.
It's about activation.

Reinvention accelerates when the world around you stops echoing who you used to be and begins reflecting who you're becoming.

Chapter 12. Find a New Signature Scent

Scent is one of the most overlooked tools of reinvention.
It bypasses logic.
It bypasses memory.
It reaches directly into identity.

A scent can transport you, elevate you, or anchor you to a moment. It can remind you of who you once were or introduce you to who you're becoming. This is why people often outgrow fragrances without even realizing it. Their body knows when a scent no longer matches their life.

Choosing a new signature scent is a quiet but powerful way to signal that you are stepping into a different era.

You don't pick it because it smells nice.
You pick it because it feels like the future.

The Psychology of Scent and Identity

Smell is processed in the same part of the brain that stores emotion, memory and instinct. This is why a single fragrance can suddenly return you to a moment you haven't thought about in decades.

And just as scent can return you to the past, it can also lead you out of it.

Reinvention is built on new cues.
New stories.
New associations.

A signature scent becomes a sensory doorway into your next chapter. Every time you wear it, your brain receives the message:

"This is who we are now."

A Story About a Bottle of Cologne and a Man Who Needed a Change

A retired firefighter once said that after twenty-five years in the same routine, he didn't know who he was without his uniform. When he left the force, he felt unmoored. His days didn't have structure, purpose or rhythm.

One afternoon at a department store, he walked past the fragrance counter. A sales clerk sprayed a cologne he had never smelled before. It was nothing like the aftershave he had worn his entire adult life.

He bought it on instinct.

For the first time in months, he felt energized. The scent didn't remind him of his past. It didn't sound like alarms, firehouse kitchens, night shifts or adrenaline. It smelled like someone who had time. Someone who was allowed to slow down. Someone who could build a new identity.

He wore it every morning.
He built new routines around that ritual — reading, walking, cooking, reconnecting with his family, taking community college classes.

He said later, "The new scent felt like permission to become someone I hadn't met yet."
That's what a signature scent can do.

Your Action Step

Choose a scent — cologne, perfume, essential oil, candle or room spray — that represents your next era. Your only rule is this:

It cannot be something from your past.

Look for scents that feel like:

- clarity
- movement
- confidence
- ease
- possibility
- creativity
- renewal
- elevation

Smell everything.
Don't rush.
Choose the one that feels aligned with the identity you're building.

And then begin wearing it intentionally.

Apply it before:

- work
- writing
- thinking
- meditation
- planning
- creative projects
- difficult conversations
- moments when you want to shift your energy

Let it mark the transition between who you've been and who you are becoming.

How ChatGPT Helps

Ask:

"Help me choose a signature scent based on the identity I'm stepping into. Describe scent families that fit my next era."

Or:

"Give me a list of scent notes associated with clarity, confidence and renewal."

Or:

"Help me create a sensory ritual around my new scent so I associate it with reinvention."

This builds a personalized blueprint that guides your choices and sharpens your intuition.

Why This Matters

Humans underestimate the power of sensory cues.
A scent can shift your nervous system faster than a motivational video, a journal entry, or a change in routine.

When you choose a fragrance that aligns with your future, you create a daily ritual of transformation. Every application becomes a reminder:

"I am stepping forward."
"I am leaving the old identity behind."
"I am allowed to change."

Reinvention is not just mental.
It's sensory.
Your new signature scent is the breath of your next chapter.

The Science of Scent and Identity

Smell is the only sense that connects *directly* to the emotional and memory centers of the brain without passing through the thinking or reasoning centers. This is why scent bypasses logic — it hits emotion first.

Here is the simple biology:

1. Scent goes straight to the limbic system

When you smell something, it travels from your nose to the **olfactory bulb**, which sits right next to two powerful parts of the brain:

- **the amygdala**, which processes emotion
- **the hippocampus**, which stores memory

This is the only sensory pathway with a direct route like this.
Every other sense — sight, sound, touch, taste — goes through the brain's "relay station" first.
Smell goes right to the emotional core.

That's why scent can:

- trigger old memories instantly
- create new emotional associations
- change your mood before you realize it
- pull you into a different version of yourself

This is also why you can smell something from childhood and immediately feel the age you were then.

2. Scent creates long-lasting memory connections

Because smell is tied directly to memory storage, scents form what neuroscientists call "associative networks." Once your brain connects a scent to an emotion or identity moment, it stays in that file forever.

That's why:

• your grandmother's perfume can feel emotional
• your grandfather's gum can feel comforting
• a childhood soap can make you feel safe
• a cologne can remind you of an entire era of your life

3. Scent can shape behavior

Studies show that scent can:

• increase focus
• reduce stress
• shift confidence
• change energy levels
• increase motivation
• trigger creativity
• regulate mood

This is why choosing a new signature scent is an identity tool, not a luxury.
You are using biology to support your reinvention.

4. Scent signals identity to others

Humans associate scent with closeness, trust, safety and attraction.
It's part of why your advice to Kevin works:
people instinctively respond to scent long before words or body language.

Chapter 13. Create or Buy One Look That Says "I'm Different Now"

Identity isn't only internal.
It is also expressed through the way you present yourself to the world. You don't need a wardrobe overhaul. You don't need a dramatic makeover. Reinvention is rarely about extremes.

You just need one look.

One outfit, one accessory, one piece of clothing that becomes the first physical expression of the next version of you. Something that feels aligned with the identity you're building and makes the old version of you pause and whisper, "We don't do that anymore."

Clothing is symbolic.
Objects carry energy.
When you wear something that represents a new era, your nervous system responds.

This is the same reason uniforms change behavior — they alter psychology.
You're not putting on a costume.
You're putting on a signal.

Why One Look Matters

Purchasing or assembling one signature look works because:

- it's manageable
- it's affordable
- it's symbolic
- it's immediate

People underestimate the psychological impact of a single intentional item, but your mind picks up every cue you give it. A new look tells your brain:

"We're stepping into something new."

You walk differently.
You speak differently.
You carry yourself differently.
You make decisions differently.

One look creates momentum.

A Story About a Woman and a Jacket That Changed Everything

There was a woman named Regina who had spent most of her career in a comfortable but unremarkable office job. She liked her coworkers. She knew her tasks well. But she felt stuck in an identity that didn't match her ambition.

One weekend she walked past a boutique and saw a tailored black jacket with structured shoulders. It was sharper, bolder, more confident than anything she owned. She didn't think she had the "right life" to wear it. It looked like something her future self would choose — not the woman she felt like now.

She tried it on anyway.

She said the moment she looked in the mirror, she felt ten percent braver.

She bought it.

On Monday she wore it to work. She sat straighter. She contributed more in the team meeting. She volunteered for a project she had been too nervous to touch for three years. Two months later her boss asked if she had ever considered a leadership program.

She didn't become a different person overnight.
But one look helped her treat herself differently.
And that treatment changed her trajectory.

One look can do that.

Your Action Step

Choose one item that symbolizes your next-era identity:

- a jacket
- a pair of shoes
- a watch
- a necklace
- a pair of glasses
- a hat
- a shirt
- a bag
- a ring
- a scarf
- a perfectly fitted pair of jeans

Something you would not have worn in your old life.
Something that represents clarity, confidence, elevation or transformation.

You don't choose it because it's trendy or extravagant.
You choose it because it feels like the future.

And then you use it intentionally:

- for important conversations
- for creative work

- for days when momentum matters
- for interviews
- for stepping into a bold decision
- for beginning something new

You become the person who wears the look, and slowly, the identity follows.

How ChatGPT Helps

Ask:

"Help me identify a signature look that reflects the identity I'm stepping into. Describe the colors, shapes and feeling of my next-era style."

Or:

"Give me five ideas for a single item that would signal a shift in my identity."

Or:

"Help me create a personal style philosophy that supports reinvention."

ChatGPT can help articulate the direction your subconscious already feels, but hasn't yet named.

Why This Matters

Reinvention isn't purely internal.
You teach your mind to shift by creating physical anchors.

When you put on something that aligns with your future self, you activate the emotional and mental traits of that identity. You begin to match the look you chose.

One look can be the beginning of a new life.
Not because of the fabric - but because of the signal.

Chapter 14. Build a Role Model Masterclass

Reinvention is easier when you stop trying to invent everything from scratch.
You are surrounded by people who already live the qualities you want to embody. They might not be celebrities or gurus. They might be ordinary people whose lives reflect something you admire.

Most transformations begin when you observe someone who represents a future you didn't know you were allowed to imagine.

A role model does not replace your identity.
They reveal new possibilities for it.

Why Studying Others Accelerates Reinvention

Humans learn by mirroring.
You absorb tone, confidence, body language, boundaries, expectations and worldview simply by observing someone who embodies qualities you want to develop.

You don't copy them.
You learn the mechanics.

This is not hero worship.
It is identity modeling.

Athletes do it.
Leaders do it.
Artists do it.
Entrepreneurs do it.
Anyone serious about reinvention does it.

You are allowed to learn from excellence.

A Story About a Quiet Man Who Found His Confidence Through Someone Else's

There was a man named Ira who worked at a hardware store for most of his adult life. He was gentle, kind and helpful, but he carried a deep lack of confidence. He wanted to speak more boldly, but decades of being overlooked had worn him down.

One day he watched a community lecture given by a local architect. The architect was not loud. He was not charismatic. He simply spoke with calm authority. He paused before answering questions. He held his shoulders evenly. He made eye contact without forcing it.

Ira wrote down the things he noticed:

- the pace of his speech
- the clarity of his words
- the steadiness of his posture
- the way he rested his hands
- the quiet certainty in his tone

He practiced these details privately. He paid attention to how it felt in his own body. He tried speaking more slowly at work. He lifted his chin when he walked. He greeted customers with more intentionality.

Within six months, he was the one people asked for when they needed real advice. Two years later he was managing the store.

He didn't become the architect.
He became the version of himself who had confidence.
A role model opened the door.
He walked through it.

Your Action Step

Make a list of five people you admire.
They can be:

- public figures
- friends
- coworkers
- people you've met only once
- creators
- authors
- leaders
- neighbors
- teachers

Then ask yourself:

- What do I admire about them?
- What do they embody that I want more of?
- How do they speak, move or make decisions?
- What habits do they practice that support their identity?
- What standards do they live by?
- What inner qualities do they demonstrate naturally?

You are not trying to become them.
You are studying the architecture of qualities that matter to you.

Pick one quality from one role model and begin practicing it in small ways.
Confidence.
Compassion.
Clarity.
Discipline.
Grace.

Boldness.
Calm strength.
Steady boundaries.
Curiosity.
Patience.
Focus.

Identity changes at the level of consistent micro-action.

How ChatGPT Helps

Ask:

"Help me analyze the qualities of a role model I admire and translate those qualities into habits I can practice."

Or:

"Give me five identity traits that define the role models I listed. Show me how to embody them slowly and realistically."

Or:

"Help me create a weekly plan to practice one quality I admire in someone else."

This turns admiration into action, and action into identity.

Why This Matters

Reinvention is not built on willpower.
It is built on intentional modeling.

You learn who you can become by observing people who already live at that level.
They show you what is possible.
They help you build the next version of yourself more quickly and

less painfully.
They remind you that you are allowed to grow beyond your history.

A role model is not someone you want to copy.
They are someone who helps you rise.

This is the quiet engine of reinvention.

Chapter 15. Say Yes to What Makes You Nervous

Reinvention always asks for a moment of courage.
Not reckless leaps.
Not dramatic reinventions overnight.
Just one simple, quiet yes to something that makes you a little uncomfortable.

Nervousness is not a sign that something is wrong.
Often, it is a sign that something new is trying to enter your life.

Your brain prefers what is familiar, even if it is limiting.
So when a new opportunity arrives, your mind may interpret it as danger, when it is actually possibility in disguise.

Most people wait to feel confident before they say yes.
But confidence is what arrives after the yes, not before it.

The Psychology Behind Nervousness

Nervousness and excitement activate the same part of the nervous system.
Your heartbeat increases.
Your breathing changes.
Your mind sharpens.

The brain then labels that sensation based on context.
If you interpret it as fear, you retreat.
If you interpret it as expansion, you move forward.

Reinvention asks you to re-label the feeling.

Instead of "I'm scared,"
try "I'm stretching."

Instead of "This is too much,"
try "This is growth."

Instead of "I can't,"
try "Maybe I can."

A Story About a Man Who Said Yes to Something Small

A man named Louis worked in finance for thirty years. He was successful, respected and stable, but he wasn't fulfilled. When his company closed, he had no idea who he was without his career.

One evening, he was invited to a community cooking class. He hadn't cooked anything more complicated than scrambled eggs in years. He almost declined. It felt silly, uncomfortable and beneath the seriousness of his situation.

His neighbor said, "Just come. You need a night out."

He said yes.

That one yes led him to meet two retired chefs who ran the class. He discovered he liked chopping vegetables. He liked the rhythm of it. He liked being a beginner at something. He liked being around people again.

Within six months, he was volunteering at a local food pantry.
Within a year, he was managing it three days a week.
He said, "That one small yes made me feel alive again."

His nervousness wasn't a warning.
It was the door.

Your Action Step

Say yes to one thing this week that makes you uncomfortable in a productive way.

Not unsafe.
Not overwhelming.
Just unfamiliar.

Examples:

- attend a class
- join a group
- introduce yourself to someone
- try an activity you've avoided
- sign up for something you've always wanted to learn
- volunteer for a small role
- go to an event alone
- share your work
- take a new route
- make a phone call you've been afraid to make

You're not chasing adrenaline.
You're building identity flexibility.

Your brain needs evidence that you are capable of stepping into the unknown and surviving it.
Every yes becomes evidence.

How ChatGPT Helps

Ask:

"Give me five opportunities in my life that I should say yes to this week based on the identity I'm building."

Or:

"Help me reframe nervousness into growth so I can take action instead of freezing."

Or:

"Create a small challenge list that stretches me without overwhelming me."

You can also ask:

"What is one action I can take today that the old version of me would avoid but the new version of me would embrace?"

This turns your nervousness into a compass.

Why This Matters

Your next identity is waiting outside your comfort zone.
Just a few steps away.
Just beyond one small yes.

Reinvention does not require boldness every day.
It requires bravery in moments.

Every yes expands you.
Every yes opens something.
Every yes adds momentum.

Nervousness is not the enemy.
It is the signal that you're heading in the right direction.

Chapter 16. Let Yourself Be Surprised

Reinvention is not a straight line.
It is not a formula.
It is a collaboration with the unknown.

You don't have to know what's coming.
You have to be willing to meet it when it arrives.

This chapter is about surprise—true, beautiful, life-altering surprise.

Not the jump-scare kind.
The soul-widening kind.
The kind that whispers:
"I didn't know I would love this."

What If You've Been Wrong About Yourself?

Most people build their identity early, then defend it for decades.

"I'm not creative."
"I'm not technical."
"I'm not good with people."
"I hate public speaking."
"I could never run a business."
"I'm not athletic."
"I don't understand money."

These are not truths.
They're survival shortcuts.
They're outdated labels, worn smooth by repetition.

What if every single one is incorrect?

What if you've underestimated yourself for years?

A Story About the Best Kind of Wrong

Nina worked as a paralegal for 25 years. She had a quiet, organized, efficient life. Her favorite part of the job was proofreading.

When she retired, she joined a local book club, then accidentally signed up for a writing workshop.

She didn't tell anyone. She almost canceled.
But the teacher was kind.
She kept going.
She wrote a few poems.
Then a story.

One day the teacher said, "You're a writer, Nina."

She cried.

It had never occurred to her.
She thought writing was for other people.
She was wrong.
Wonderfully, entirely, delightfully wrong

She's now working on a book.
Not for fame.
Not for sales.
For herself.

Because she gets to be surprised by who she still is.

Your Action Step

Let something surprise you this week. Let yourself be wrong in a beautiful way.

Try something you've secretly wanted to try but assumed you'd be bad at.

Let go of needing to be good.
Let go of needing to know.

The point is not to be perfect.
The point is to wake up a sleeping part of yourself.

Try:

- a class or tutorial you've always skipped
- skctching somcthing poorly and posting it anyway
- making a short video even if you're camera-shy
- speaking in front of a small group
- trying a new format or tool
- learning a skill with no career payoff
- reading a book on a subject you've ignored
- talking to someone in a field you admire

You are not done discovering who you are.
You're not even close.

What to Ask ChatGPT

"Show me five things I've probably been wrong about in my self-assessment."

Or:

"Help me build a short list of things I might secretly be great at if I gave myself permission."

Or:

"What could surprise me this year if I dropped my old labels?"

Let your AI assistant help you see what you've been too close to see.

Why This Matters

Reinvention is not just a fix.
It's a rediscovery.

You are not here to play out the same personality forever.

The most alive people are the ones still being surprised by their own story.

You don't have to be right about yourself.
You only have to stay curious.

Let yourself be surprised.
Let yourself be found.

There is more in you than you know.

Chapter 17. Build an Inner Circle That Lifts Your Future, Not Your Past

Reinvention is not done alone.
Not because you *can't* do it alone, but because the people around you shape the speed and direction of your evolution more than you realize.

Most people stay stuck because they surround themselves with people who love the *old* version of them.
People who depend on that version.
People who feel safer when you don't grow.

If your circle benefits more from your stagnation than your success, you don't have a circle.
You have an anchor.

This chapter is about rebuilding the people strategy of your life.

The Three Groups You Meet When You Start Changing

As soon as you shift, three types of people show up.

1. The "Why Are You Changing?" Crowd

They aren't villains.
They're just invested in the old script.
Your change forces them to confront their own inertia.

They say things like:
"You're acting different."
"You've changed."
"What's going on with you?"

"You used to be more fun."
"I liked the old you."

Translation:
"I'm uncomfortable because your evolution highlights my lack of it."

They fade out on their own if you stop explaining yourself.

2. The "Good for You, But Not for Me" People

These folks clap politely, but at a distance.
They won't sabotage you.
They won't support you either.
They're neutral observers in your story.

Let them be neutral.
They are not your builders.
They are not your brakes.
They're background scenery.

3. The Builders

These are rare and unmistakable.
They don't question your change.
They don't compete with it.
They don't shrink from it.

Builders widen the space around you so you can grow into it.

They say things like:
"How can I help?"
"You're not crazy. You're early."
"That idea has legs. Let's explore it."
"I see your next chapter clearly. Want to talk it through?"

Builders hold a flashlight to your future, not your past.

Why This Matters for Reinvention

Identity grows faster in an environment that can hold it.
If everyone around you treats you like a past version of yourself, it becomes harder to step into the next one.

Reinvention requires three things:

- space
- support
- reflection

Your inner circle is the ecosystem that supplies all three.

A Story About Choosing the Right People

Lorenzo spent forty years running a barbecue restaurant. When he retired, he wasn't sure who he was without the apron, the smoke, and the regulars shouting his name.

His friends kept telling him to "just relax" and "take it easy" because that's who they thought he was.

But he didn't want to sit.
He wanted to learn photography.

He joined a small evening class where the group was full of twenty- and thirty-year-olds who knew more about shutter speed than he'd ever know.

On the first day, a young woman looked at his camera and said, "Vintage. Cool. You're going to make art with that."

No one had ever linked him to the word *art* before.

Six months later, he had a small exhibition at the library.

Reinvention isn't magic.
It's environment.

When you sit next to people who see you as capable, creative, and evolving, you start to believe it too.

Your Action Step

Take inventory of your circle.

Write these three lists:

1. The people who keep you tied to your past
2. The people who stay neutral
3. The people who lift your future

Then make one decision:

Spend more time with builders.
Even one or two can reshape your trajectory.

This is not about cutting everyone else out.
It's about recalibrating who gets access to your inner world.

You deserve a circle that reflects your next chapter.

What to Ask ChatGPT

"Help me evaluate whether the people in my life support the future I want."

Or:

"Help me craft a script for setting new boundaries with people who keep dragging me back into old patterns."

Or:

"Show me what a healthier inner circle would look like based on my reinvention goals."

AI cannot choose your people.
But it can help you see them clearly.

Why This Matters

You do not rise alone.
You rise with the people who refuse to let you shrink.

Reinvention is a relationship decision as much as a personal one.
Choose people who speak to your potential, not your limitations.

The right circle makes reinvention inevitable.

Chapter 18. Rewrite the Story You Have Been Carrying

Every reinvention begins with a story ending.

Not the dramatic kind.
The quiet kind.
The story you have repeated so many times that you don't even notice you're telling it anymore.

The story that shaped the choices you made.
The story that built your fears.
The story that made your world smaller in ways you never meant it to be.

You know exactly which story I mean.
The one that starts with "I've always been the type who…"
or "That's just the way my life went…"
or "After what happened, I never…"
or "I guess I'm just someone who can't…"

We inherit these narratives without choosing them.
Sometimes from a parent.
Sometimes from an ex.
Sometimes from a failure.
Sometimes from a childhood moment no one else remembers but shaped everything.

Reinvention demands that you examine the script you've been acting out and ask one bold question:

Is it even true?

Most people live inside a story they never edited.

This chapter is where you take the pen back.

The Story That Shapes You vs. the Story You Choose Now

There are two kinds of stories:

1. The story of origin
Where you came from.
What shaped you.
What you survived.
What you learned.

This story is valid.
It deserves respect.
It holds the truth of your lived experience.

But it is not the map of your future unless you decide it is.

2. The story of identity
Who you believe yourself to be now.
What you think you're allowed to want.
How you believe life works for you.
What you think you deserve.

This story is optional.
This is the one you rewrite.

Most people mix the two and never question the merge.

Reinvention is the moment you separate them.

A Story That Proves This Point

Nina grew up being told she was "the shy one."
Every teacher. Every relative. Every friend.

Even at forty-six, she introduced herself by saying, "I'm shy," as if it were her last name.

When she joined a ceramics class after a divorce, the instructor asked if anyone wanted to share their work in the upcoming community showcase.

Nina stepped back.
Of course she did.
Shy people don't stand in front of crowds.

But the instructor, who knew nothing about her history, said, "You're not shy. You're observant and precise. You'd be amazing up there."

That one sentence cracked the shell of her old story.

She entered the showcase.

She received a standing ovation for her piece.

No one in that audience knew she was "shy."
Because she no longer was.

She had been living inside a story written in childhood by people who barely understood her.

You cannot become who you want to be while holding a story built for the person you used to be.

Your Action Step: Two Versions of One Moment

Choose one story that has held you back.
One memory, belief or identity label that has followed you for years.

Then write two paragraphs:

Paragraph 1: The story as you have always told it.
What happened.
What hurt.
What it made you believe about yourself.

Paragraph 2: The story as you choose to see it now.
What you learned.
What strength it built.
How it shaped your capacity, resilience or creativity.
Why it does not define you anymore.

This is a powerful exercise.
It gives you authorship again.

You will feel the shift immediately.

What to Ask ChatGPT

Here is where AI becomes a tool for rewriting identity in a grounded, safe way.

Try prompts like:

- "Help me rewrite a limiting story I have carried for years into a version that empowers me."
- "Show me what this past experience might look like if I reframed it through strength instead of shame."
- "Turn this painful memory into a growth chapter that supports my reinvention goals."

AI does not erase the past.
It helps you reinterpret it so the past stops dictating the future.

Why This Chapter Matters

People think reinvention is about a new hairstyle, a new job or a new relationship.

It isn't.

Reinvention is changing the story your life is built on.
When you change the story, the choices change.
When the choices change, the future changes.

This chapter is the hinge.
It separates who you were from who you are becoming.

You cannot move forward while telling a story that holds you back.

Rewrite it.
Choose again.
Step into the version of you that the old story never allowed.

Chapter 19. Make Daily Non-Negotiables a Declaration of Life

Reinvention is not a dramatic moment.
It is not the big decision.
It is the dozen small decisions you make when no one is watching.

Most people underestimate the power of the quiet choices.
They imagine transformation as a sweeping gesture, a cinematic change, a bold leap.

But reinvention is built in the invisible hours.

The moment you choose the glass of water instead of the scroll.
The moment you choose a walk instead of worry.
The moment you choose a new thought instead of the old reflex.
The moment you close the computer and say, "No more chaos today."
The moment you choose rest instead of guilt.
The moment you choose purpose over autopilot.

Daily non-negotiables are not tasks.
They are declarations.

Every time you honor one, you reinforce a new identity.

This is who I am now.
This is what I do.
This is how I care for myself.
This is how I shape my days.
This is how I move toward the person I am becoming.

They are the discipline of becoming.

The Hidden Architecture of Change

Life is built in layers.

The outer layer is what the world sees.
The inner layer is what you privately choose.

When you shift the inner layer, the outer layer eventually moves.

It cannot stay the same.

This is why non-negotiables work.
They quietly alter the internal architecture of your life, which eventually changes the external structure without force.

Think of them as internal votes.

Each one tells your brain:

- I am trustworthy
- I am not stuck
- I can build momentum
- I can be consistent
- I am worth the effort

These are not small messages.
They rewire identity.

Another Story: The Woman Who Found Herself After a Layoff

At fifty-eight, Janelle lost her job when her department closed.
She had been with the company for thirty-two years.
Her first reaction was panic.
Her second reaction was shame.
Her third reaction was isolation.

She stayed in bed.
She avoided calls.
She blamed herself.

One morning, after crying in the shower, she sat on the edge of the tub and whispered, "I can't let this be the end of me."

She picked up an old notebook and wrote:

**Today I will:

1. Go outside
2. Read something meaningful
3. Do one thing that moves my life forward**

It didn't feel like much.
But for the first time in weeks, she had a direction.

The next day, she repeated it.
The day after that, she changed the list slightly.
After a week, she added a new non-negotiable: "Apply for one job or opportunity."
After a month, she was volunteering at a local arts center.
After three months, she joined a watercolor class.
After six months, she had a part-time job teaching creative writing to seniors.
After one year, she described herself as "a new woman."

No dramatic moment launched her transformation.
It was the small, steady honoring of her non-negotiables that rebuilt her self-worth and her sense of direction.

This is the magic of daily standards.
They bring you back to yourself.

Your Non-Negotiables Should Be Simple but Identity-Shifting

A non-negotiable is not a chore.
It is an act of alignment.

It should:

- Strengthen your next identity
- Establish emotional stability
- Reduce decision fatigue
- Build inner safety
- Support your signature goal
- Prove to you that you follow through

Each one is a micro-commitment that says, "My future matters enough to act on it today."

You Only Need Three to Start

Here are examples across different identities:

For someone reinventing after burnout:
- Drink water first
- Ten minutes of breath or quiet
- Do one thing slowly on purpose

For someone reinventing after divorce:
- One self-kindness action
- One personal expansion (book, walk, class)
- One boundary honored

For someone reinventing in retirement:
- Move your body

- Learn something new
- Make something with your hands

For someone reinventing creatively:

- Capture one idea
- Practice your craft for ten minutes
- Study one person who inspires you

The simplicity is the power.

Reinvention Without Self-Trust Fails

Daily non-negotiables build the most essential ingredient in reinvention:
self-trust.

Without it, change collapses.
With it, change compounds.

When you keep a promise to yourself every day, even a tiny one, your brain begins to believe you again.

That belief unlocks everything.

Let ChatGPT Support Your Non-Negotiables

Use AI to make this part easier, not heavier.

Try:

- "Help me create three non-negotiables that support the future I want."
- "Rewrite my daily habits so they reflect my next identity."

• "Create a daily check-in question that keeps me aligned."
• "Give me micro-routines that reduce chaos and increase clarity."

AI becomes your accountability tool, your planner and your mirror.

Your Action Step: Claim Your Three Today

Right now, choose:

1. One non-negotiable for your body
2. One non-negotiable for your mind
3. One non-negotiable for your future

When you honor them tomorrow, your reinvention has already begun.

Not because the actions are big.
But because they are yours.

This chapter is where you learn that transformation is not about force.
It is about consistency, clarity and claiming the small actions that build a new life from the inside out.

Your non-negotiables are the evidence of your evolution.

Chapter 20. Surround Yourself With Beauty, Inside and Out

Reinvention is not an inner journey alone.
Your environment speaks.
Your surroundings shape your mood, your expectations, your imagination and your courage to live differently.

People underestimate how deeply space affects identity.

A cluttered home creates a cluttered mind.
A lifeless room creates a lifeless outlook.
An uninspiring environment weakens the courage needed to change.
And a space filled with relics of who you used to be keeps you loyal to a life you are outgrowing.

Beauty is not decoration.
Beauty is nourishment.

This chapter is about choosing an environment that supports the person you are becoming, not the person you have been.

The Science of Why Beauty Matters

Environmental psychology has studied this for decades.

When people spend time in beautiful environments, even small ones:

- Stress levels fall
- Creativity increases
- Problem solving improves
- Emotional resilience strengthens
- Decision-making gets clearer
- Purpose becomes easier to sustain

Even simple beauty has this effect:

A vase of flowers.
A candle with a warm glow.
A clean desk.
A photo of a place you love.
A corner that feels like a refuge.

Beauty is not indulgent.
Beauty is fuel.

A Story: The Woman Who Reinvented Herself One Shelf at a Time

When Myra turned sixty, she told a friend, "I feel like my life ended ten years ago and I forgot to get the memo."

Divorced.
Grown children living far away.
An empty house full of old memories.
Every room reminded her of a version of herself she no longer recognized.

One night, she sat on the couch and whispered, "I don't want to live in a museum of my past."

The next day, she cleared one shelf in her living room. Just one.

She removed everything.
She dusted.
She added a plant, a framed picture from a recent trip, and one small sculpture she had always loved but never displayed.

When she stepped back, she felt something lift.

A sense of possibility.
A tiny spark.

She cleared another shelf the next week.
Then a drawer.
Then a closet.
Then a room.

Over six months, her home became a reflection of who she was becoming.

She later said, "Changing my space changed my story. I didn't expect that."

Your surroundings whisper to you every day.
Make sure they whisper toward your future.

Beauty Is Not Expensive. It Is Intentional.

You don't need renovations or designer anything.
Reinvention is built on intention, not price.

Here are simple beauty upgrades that matter:

- Clean one surface
- Remove one item that feels heavy or outdated
- Add light where a space feels dim
- Bring in one living thing, like a plant or fresh herbs
- Replace something worn with something that sparks joy
- Use a scent that uplifts you
- Display objects that remind you of your future, not your past
- Add color where your life feels muted
- Frame something meaningful
- Make one corner of your home a sanctuary

Beauty is not about perfection.
It is about alignment.

Your Outer Space Reflects Your Inner Pace

If you want a calmer life, soften your environment.
If you want a creative life, add color.
If you want a bigger life, clear space.
If you want to feel alive again, add movement, scent, texture, sound.

This chapter gives you permission to stop tolerating environments that drain you.

Your space should help you rise, not hold you down.

What to Ask ChatGPT

Let AI help you design your next-era environment.

Try:

• "Help me redesign one corner of my home to reflect my next identity."
• "Give me simple beauty upgrades that cost under twenty dollars."
• "Help me create an uplifting morning environment with scent, sound and color."
• "Give me a new vision for my bedroom based on calm and clarity."
• "Show me how to declutter without overwhelm."

Your environment becomes a collaborator in your reinvention.

Your Action Step: Curate One Square Foot

Reinvention doesn't start with the whole room.
It starts with one small space.

Choose one square foot today.
A shelf.
A drawer.
A corner.
A bedside table.

Clear it.
Clean it.
Make it beautiful.
Make it supportive.
Make it yours.

Tomorrow, choose another.

Beauty builds momentum.
Momentum builds identity.

Your next chapter deserves a space that honors it.

Chapter 21. Be Seen, Even If It's Messy

Reinvention is not a private act.
It begins alone, but it becomes real only when you allow yourself to be witnessed.

Most people try to change in secret.
They hide the work.
They hide the effort.
They hide the vulnerability.
They hide the early steps because they're not polished yet.
They hide themselves until they feel "ready."

But here's the truth no one says out loud:

If you wait to be perfect before being seen, you will never be seen at all.

This chapter is the invitation to step into the light before you feel finished, before you feel prepared, before you feel confident, and before you know exactly who you are becoming.

Because reinvention requires visibility.

Not the performative kind.
The honest kind.

Why Being Seen Is Terrifying and Necessary

Most people fear being seen for one reason:
Visibility exposes truth.

If you show up in the world as yourself:

- Someone may misjudge you
- Someone may misunderstand you
- Someone may not like the new version of you
- Someone may remember the old you
- Someone may have opinions you never asked for

But the deeper fear is this:

If you are seen, you might discover who you truly are.
And once you know, you cannot unknow.
You cannot go back.

But here is the part people forget:
Visibility is also how you attract the life that fits you.

You cannot call in aligned people, opportunities, work, friendships or love by staying hidden.

To be found, you must be seen.
Even if it's messy.

A Story: The Man Who Started Showing Up Online at Fifty-Four

Elliot had always been the quiet one.
Good at his job, kind to his coworkers, safe, invisible.

After his divorce, he told a friend, "I feel like I've lived half a life."

She said, "Then live the other half out loud."

He didn't know what that meant, so she signed him up for a beginner photography class.
One assignment required him to post a single photo on a private group forum and write one sentence about it.

He almost didn't do it.
He didn't want to look foolish.
He didn't want anyone to judge his work.
He didn't want to expose how unsure he felt.

But he posted the photo.

It got two comments.
Both kind.

He posted another the next week.
Then another.
Then he started adding captions that were more personal.

Within six months, his work was being shared.
Within a year, he had a small but engaged audience.
Within two years, he was exhibiting at a local gallery.

He always said, "My life didn't change when I picked up a camera. It changed when I allowed myself to be seen holding it."

That is the essence of this chapter.

The Lie of the Polished Life

Every great transformation you admire began messy.

Messy writing.
Messy first attempts.
Messy early ideas.
Messy emotions.
Messy conversations.
Messy boundaries.

Messy versions of confidence.
Messy courage.

People become polished only after they allow themselves to be imperfect in public long enough to learn who they are.

Messy is the birthplace of mastery.

Where You Can Begin Being Seen

You don't have to broadcast your deepest truth to the world.
You only need to practice visibility in small, gentle ways.

Try one of these:

- Share one honest sentence with a friend
- Post one small piece of work on social media
- Tell someone you trust that you are reinventing
- Show up to a class even if you feel unsure
- Join a group where no one knows your history
- Speak up once during a meeting or gathering
- Ask for help before you are desperate
- Say what you want out loud
- Let someone compliment you without deflecting
- Take a selfie on a day you do not feel perfect and keep it
- Show up in a space where the old you would never go

Visibility is not a performance.
It is permission.

What to Ask ChatGPT

AI can help you ease into being seen.

Try:

• "Help me express something honest about myself in a simple way."
• "Guide me in writing a short post that reflects who I am becoming."
• "Give me confidence phrases that help me show up even when I feel messy."
• "Help me practice being visible while staying true to myself."

This is not about becoming loud.
It is about becoming real.

Your Action Step: Share One Thing Today

Choose one tiny act of visibility:

A sentence.
A thought.
A photo.
A message.
A creative piece.
A moment of truth.
A small request.
A small reveal.

Choose something that says, "Here I am, evolving."

Reinvention accelerates when you stop hiding from yourself and stop hiding from the world.

Being seen is not a risk.
It is a doorway.

Walk through it.

Chapter 22. Put the Phone Down and Live Your Life

Modern life has a way of shrinking our world without us noticing.

One message becomes three.
Three becomes twelve.
A quick check becomes an hour.
An hour becomes a habit.
A habit becomes a default way of living.

We tell ourselves we're "staying connected," but often we're drifting further from our real life.
From our own thoughts.
From our body.
From our relationships.
From our creativity.
From the world around us.
From our next chapter.

Reinvention demands presence.
And presence requires putting the phone down.

This chapter is not about judgment.
It is about reclaiming your life from the endless pull of attention that keeps you from the life you are trying to build.

The Truth We Don't Want to Admit

The phone is not the enemy.
Distraction is.

Every notification, every update, every alert is a tiny door that pulls you out of your life.

And when you are reinventing yourself, your life needs you in it.

Your attention is the currency of your identity.
Where it goes, your future follows.

This chapter invites you to take that currency back.

A Story: The Woman Who Lived Online Until She Didn't Recognize Herself

Dana worked in tech for decades.
Brilliant.
Capable.
Always reachable.
Always efficient.
Always exhausted.

Her days were chopped into digital fragments.
Messages. Alerts. Pings.
A life lived in one-minute increments.

After her second burnout, her therapist asked her a simple question:

"When was the last time you were bored?"

She couldn't answer.

She had forgotten what it felt like to hear her own thoughts without interruption.
To sit in silence.
To experience a moment without documenting it.

To enjoy something without announcing it.
To feel her life instead of managing it.

She decided to do a thirty-day experiment.
Every day she would take one hour completely offline.

No phone.
No computer.
No TV.
No background noise.

The first few days were uncomfortable.
Her mind twitched like a phantom limb reaching for a device.

But by the second week she felt something she had not felt in years: calm.

By the third week she felt more:
direction.

By the end of the month, she said, "I feel like I met myself again."

Her reinvention began not with a big idea, but with one hour of silence.

This is the power of putting the phone down.

Why Presence Is Necessary for Reinvention

Your future self cannot appear in a crowded mind.

To reinvent yourself, you need:

• Quiet
• Space
• Reflection

- Curiosity
- Creativity
- Emotional clarity
- A sense of your own desires
- A connection to your inner voice

These things cannot survive in a constant storm of notifications.

When you reduce digital noise, your inner world becomes audible again.

You begin to hear:

- What you want
- What you don't want
- What you are tired of
- What you dream about
- What you're ready to walk away from
- What you're ready to walk toward

Reinvention is not a search for answers.
It is removing the noise that keeps you from hearing them.

A Moment That Belongs Only to You

There is a kind of sacredness in giving yourself uninterrupted time.

One walk without your phone
One meal without your screen
One morning without news
One evening without scrolling
One creative session without distraction
One conversation where your full attention is present

Presence is a magnet.
It attracts clarity.
It attracts ideas.
It attracts peace.
It attracts your future self.

What to Ask ChatGPT

Use AI to help you design a healthier relationship with your digital world.

Try:

• "Help me create a gentle digital detox plan that doesn't feel punishing."
• "Give me offline activities that nurture creativity and calm."
• "Help me set healthy boundaries with my phone so I can be more present."
• "Give me a script for telling people I'm less available because I'm reinventing."

AI can support your life, but it cannot substitute for living it.

This chapter reminds you that reinvention requires moments when the only voice you hear is your own.

Your Action Step: Claim One Offline Window Today

Choose one window of time:

10 minutes
20 minutes

30 minutes
1 hour

Put your phone in another room.
Close your laptop.
Step into your life.

Notice:

- What thoughts come up
- What you feel in your body
- What you remember
- What new ideas appear
- What you want next
- How different the world feels without interruption

You don't need to escape your life to reinvent it.
You only need to step back into it.

Your next chapter is waiting for your attention.
Give it space to arrive.

Chapter 23. Refuse to Apologize for Your Evolution

There comes a moment in every reinvention when you must make a decision that feels both freeing and uncomfortable:

You stop apologizing for becoming the person you were always meant to be.

This is the chapter where you claim your right to grow.
Your right to change.
Your right to expand.
Your right to leave things behind.
Your right to want more.
Your right to shed expectations placed on you by people who didn't know your full story.
Your right to design a life that feels like your own.

Reinvention requires unapologetic ownership.

Not arrogance.
Not defiance.
Not rebellion for the sake of rebellion.

Clarity.
Confidence.
Self-respect.

You are not required to shrink so others stay comfortable.

Why People Apologize for Changing

People apologize for evolving because:

- Someone might not approve
- Someone might misinterpret the change
- Someone might miss the old version of you
- Someone might say "you've changed" like it's an insult
- Someone might pressure you back into familiar patterns
- Someone might guilt you into staying small
- Someone might project their fears onto your growth

But these concerns are rooted in one truth:

People who benefit from your old identity often resist your new one.

And that is not your problem.

Reinvention requires courage.
Courage requires boundaries.
Boundaries require unapologetic ownership of who you are becoming.

A Story: The Woman Who Outgrew Her Entire Circle

For twenty years, Priya was the caretaker of her family and friends.
Always available.
Always helpful.
Always exhausted.

After a health scare at fifty-two, she realized she had spent decades living as a supporting character in everyone else's life.

She started making changes.

She said no more often.
She took long morning walks.

She joined a pottery class.
She stepped away from draining friendships.
She paid for coaching to understand what she truly wanted.
She began writing again.

She never made a dramatic announcement.
She didn't post about it.
She didn't hold a meeting.

She simply changed.

Some people were thrilled.
Some drifted away.
Some became suspicious.
Some became resentful.
Some said, "You're not the same. What happened to you?"

Her answer?

"I stopped apologizing for wanting a life."

It was the first honest sentence she had spoken in years.

People who loved her adjusted.
People who didn't were never meant to stay.

This is the cost and the gift of evolution.

You Are Allowed to Change Without Explaining Yourself

You don't owe anyone:

- A justification
- A defense
- A permission slip

- A presentation
- A promise to go back
- A reassurance that the old you is still there

You are allowed to change simply because you want to.

Evolution is natural.
Stagnation is not.

If someone cannot hold space for your growth, they cannot hold space for your future.

This chapter gives you permission to stop negotiating your expansion.

Where Unapologetic Growth Shows Up

You will notice it in small places:

- Your voice gets clearer
- Your opinions get calmer
- Your boundaries become firmer
- Your home becomes more aligned
- Your clothes feel more like you
- Your priorities shift
- Your tolerance for chaos falls
- Your desire for peace rises
- Your confidence stops needing external approval

Unapologetic evolution is subtle.
It is not loud.
It is not flashy.
It is a quiet, steady alignment between your inner world and outer life.

What to Ask ChatGPT

Let AI support you in articulating your evolution with strength and clarity.

Try:

• "Help me put words to the new version of myself without apologizing for it."
• "Help me express a boundary with calm confidence."
• "Give me phrases that reflect my unapologetic growth."
• "Help me write a script for stepping into my next chapter with clarity."

This book uses AI as a mirror, not a permission slip.

Your Action Step: Change One Thing Without Explaining

Choose one thing today that reflects your evolution and do it without apology.

• Wear something bold
• Post something honest
• Say no to something draining
• Say yes to something new
• End one obligation you have outgrown
• Start something that lights you up
• Rearrange one corner of your home
• Change your schedule to suit you

Do it without long explanation, without self-deprecation, without overthinking.

Step into your next chapter like someone who knows their evolution is valid.

Because it is.

Chapter 24. Stop Seeking Validation From People Who Never Gave It Before

Every reinvention eventually hits this crossroads:
You must decide whose approval you are no longer willing to chase.

This chapter is where most people stumble, because this is the moment when reinvention becomes real.
It forces you to confront history.
Patterns.
Family dynamics.
Old friendships.
Old wounds.
Old stories about worth.
Old habits of shrinking for someone else's comfort.

You cannot become a new version of yourself while constantly looking backward for applause from people who never clapped in the first place.

Reinvention requires a shift in where your validation comes from.

And sometimes that means walking away from places you have always gone for approval that never arrived.

Why This Is One of the Hardest Parts of Reinvention

People look for validation in familiar places, even when those places have never been generous.

Why?

Because the human heart loves patterns.
It gravitates toward what it knows.
Even painful patterns feel safer than unfamiliar freedom.

This is why people seek approval from:

- The parent who never praised them
- The ex who couldn't see their value
- The friend who only shows up for gossip or crisis
- The boss who withholds support
- The colleague who always minimizes their talent
- The sibling who treats them like the family punchline
- The old circle that remembers only the old version of them

Here is the truth:

Seeking validation from someone who has never given it is emotional quicksand.
No matter how hard you try, you do not move forward.

Reinvention requires letting that go.

A Story: The Man Who Stopped Trying to Impress His Brother

Daniel spent forty years trying to earn his older brother's approval.
No matter what Daniel accomplished, his brother dismissed it.

When Daniel bought a house, his brother said he overpaid.
When Daniel earned a promotion, his brother said it was "luck."
When Daniel started painting as a hobby, his brother said it was "a phase."
When Daniel lost weight, his brother said it wouldn't last.

Every achievement was met with a shrug.

Daniel's turning point came during a family reunion.
His brother made another cutting remark about Daniel's work, and Daniel felt something inside him finally break.

Not in a painful way, but in a freeing way.

He walked outside, sat alone on a bench and whispered to himself:

"I have spent my entire life trying to impress someone who is not capable of being impressed."

That moment became the start of his reinvention.

Over the next year:

He stopped explaining his choices
He stopped seeking praise
He stopped taking the bait
He stopped shrinking
He stopped sharing his dreams with people who could not hold them

He later said, "When I stopped chasing his validation, my life started."

When you stop chasing the approval of the wrong people, the right path appears.

Reinvention Requires a New Source of Validation

Validation should come from:

• Your own integrity
• Your own progress

- Your daily non-negotiables
- Your growth
- Your peace
- Your alignment with your next identity
- People who have earned the right to hear your dreams
- People who celebrate your expansion
- Communities that support your reinvention
- Mentors who see your potential
- Environments that match who you are becoming

Your new life cannot be built with old approval systems.

What to Ask ChatGPT

Use AI to shift your frame around validation and self-worth.

Try:

- "Help me detach from seeking approval from people who never supported me."
- "Give me healthier sources of validation for the person I'm becoming."
- "Help me rewrite the story I tell myself when someone minimizes my growth."
- "Give me internal validation phrases that strengthen my confidence."

Reinvention doesn't require external applause.
It requires internal alignment.

Your Action Step: Seek Validation From a New Source Today

Choose one of these:

- Praise yourself for something honest
- Share your growth with someone who celebrates you
- Stop explaining a decision to someone who doesn't deserve that explanation
- End a conversation that drains your energy
- Choose silence over defending your evolution
- Tell yourself, out loud, "I do not need their approval to move forward"
- Write down five ways your life is better now than it was a year ago

Validation is not about ego.
It is about direction.

When you stop seeking it from the wrong people, your life expands.

Your confidence grows.
Your energy rises.
Your path clears.
Your reinvention accelerates.

This chapter is where you end the chase that never brought you peace and step fully into the life that does.

Chapter 25. Start the Thing You've Been Putting Off for Years

Every person carries a silent list.

The project they always wanted to start.
The dream they never gave time to.
The book they meant to write.
The business they meant to launch.
The class they meant to take.
The conversation they meant to have.
The boundary they meant to set.
The life shift they kept planning for "someday."

Reinvention has no patience for "someday."

This chapter asks one powerful question:

What have you been putting off for years that would change your life if you started it today?

And then it asks an even more powerful one:

Why not now?

The Psychology of Delay

People don't delay because they're lazy.
They delay because:

- The dream feels too big
- The risk feels too real
- The old identity feels too tight
- The fear of being seen feels too uncomfortable

- Someone once minimized their ambition
- They convinced themselves it wasn't the right time
- Life's emergencies always came first
- They didn't know where to start
- The thought of failing felt unbearable
- The thought of succeeding felt even scarier

Delay is often self-protection disguised as procrastination.

But reinvention requires choosing courage over delay.

A Story: The Man Who Waited Thirty Years to Start His Dream

Malcolm had always wanted to write a novel.
He started dozens of times.
He wrote outlines on napkins.
He filled notebooks with ideas.
He read every book on writing.
He took one workshop.
Then waited.
And waited.
And waited.

At sixty-four, after losing a dear friend unexpectedly, he had a moment of clarity.

He said to himself, "If I don't start now, I never will."

He committed to writing one page a day.
Not ten.
Not five.
One.

At the end of the year, he had a manuscript.
At the end of the next year, he had an agent.
At sixty-seven, he signed his first book deal.

He later said, "The hardest part wasn't the writing. It was giving myself permission to begin."

Your reinvention may hinge on permission you've withheld from yourself for far too long.

What Have You Delayed?

Ask yourself:

- What idea has followed me for years?
- What dream keeps tapping me on the shoulder?
- What project makes my heart race when I imagine completing it?
- What would my life look like if I finally started?
- What am I afraid will happen if I do?
- What am I afraid will happen if I don't?

Every reinvention has a pressure point.
This chapter helps you find it.

You Don't Have to Start Big. You Just Have to Start.

People think starting requires momentum.
It doesn't.

Starting creates momentum.

Choose the smallest version of the thing you've been delaying:

- One paragraph
- One sketch
- One phone call
- One email
- One application
- One class
- One request
- One batch of supplies
- One hour
- One step

You don't need a plan.
You need a beginning.

What to Ask ChatGPT

AI can remove the overwhelm from starting.

Try:

- "Help me take the first step toward my long-delayed dream."
- "Give me a simple plan to begin the project I've been avoiding."
- "Break my big dream into ten tiny steps."
- "Help me understand why I've delayed this and how to move past it."
- "Write me a commitment plan based on my next identity."

ChatGPT becomes your partner in beginning, not your judge.

Your Action Step: Begin the First Ten Minutes Today

Choose something you've delayed for years.
Set a timer for ten minutes.
Begin.

Not perfectly.
Not boldly.
Not impressively.

Begin as a declaration of identity:

"I am someone who moves toward the life I want."

Ten minutes today becomes twenty tomorrow.
Twenty becomes momentum.
Momentum becomes pride.
Pride becomes clarity.
Clarity becomes transformation.

Your reinvention is waiting at the starting line.

Cross it.

Chapter 26. Say Yes to What Makes You Nervous

Reinvention is not built on comfort.
It is built on edges.
The edges where your heart races a little faster.
Where your palms warm.
Where your thoughts wobble between excitement and fear.
Where you feel the pull forward and the pull backward at the same time.

Most people run from those edges.
You will not.
Because reinvention requires stepping into experiences that stretch your identity.

This chapter is about saying yes to the things that make you nervous, not because fear disappears, but because the person you are becoming lives on the other side of that yes.

The Role of Discomfort in Becoming Someone New

Discomfort is not a sign to stop.
It is a sign that something new is happening.

When you feel nervous:

- Your brain is rewriting patterns
- Your routines are being disrupted
- Your identity is shifting
- Your potential is being activated
- Your life is opening

We tend to misinterpret nervousness as danger, but often it is just unfamiliarity.
Your body reacts the same way to excitement and fear.
The difference is the story you attach to the feeling.

Reinvention requires choosing the story that expands you.

A Story: The Woman Who Took a Class That Terrified Her

At fifty-nine, Delilah had talked herself out of trying yoga for twenty years.

She thought:

"I'm not flexible."
"Everyone else will know what they're doing."
"I'll look silly."
"I'll be the oldest person there."
"I won't belong."

Her daughter eventually convinced her to try one beginner class.
Delilah agreed only because she thought canceling would be rude.

When she walked into the studio, her hands trembled.
When the instructor said, "Welcome," Delilah almost turned around.
But she stayed.

The first thirty minutes were awkward.
Her balance wobbled.
Her breath was shallow.
Her nerves were loud.

But halfway through, something shifted.
Her body softened.
Her mind quieted.
Her fear loosened.

At the end of class, she cried.
Not because it was hard, but because it was the first time in years she felt alive.

She now goes three times a week.
She says yes to more things than she says no to.
Her world expanded because she took one nervous step.

This is how reinvention works.

Your Nervous Yes Is a Compass

Ask yourself:

- What is one thing I secretly want to do that makes me nervous?
- What opportunity have I been talking myself out of?
- What experience feels both exciting and intimidating?
- What small leap would make me proud?
- What would the next version of me say yes to?

Your nervous yes is pointing to your next life.

Examples of Nervous Yes Moments

- Attending an event alone
- Posting something honest
- Signing up for a class
- Pitching your work

- Sharing your art
- Wearing something bold
- Traveling somewhere new
- Trying a new skill
- Ending a long-outgrown commitment
- Asking for help
- Asking for more
- Speaking up in a room where you usually stay quiet
- Saying yes to joy after a long season of survival

Your yes does not have to be loud.
It only has to be chosen.

What to Ask ChatGPT

AI can help you navigate nervous decisions with clarity.

Try:

- "Help me understand why this opportunity makes me nervous and why it might be worth doing."
- "List five possible outcomes if I say yes to this new experience."
- "Help me prepare for a situation that scares me in a healthy way."
- "Give me a confidence script for stepping outside my comfort zone."

You don't have to leap alone.
You can be supported.

Your Action Step: Say One Nervous Yes This Week

Choose something small.
Small is enough.

- Attend the event
- Join the class
- Post the thing
- Make the call
- Share your work
- Send the application
- Book the trip
- Try the activity

Your nervous yes is the doorway to your next identity.

Say it.
Walk through it.
Let it reshape you.

Chapter 27. Study the People You Admire Like It's a Masterclass

Reinvention does not happen in isolation.
You rise faster when you study people who already embody traits, habits or mindsets you want for your next chapter.

Admiration is a compass.
Pay attention to who pulls your attention forward.
Pay attention to who makes you think, "That's possible for me."
Pay attention to who triggers a quiet spark of envy or inspiration.
Both are clues.

This chapter teaches you how to turn admiration into transformation.

Why Admiration Matters

The people you admire reveal your future, not your past.

If you pay attention, you will notice patterns:

You admire calm people when you crave peace.
You admire bold people when you crave courage.
You admire creative people when you crave expression.
You admire leaders when you crave agency.
You admire grounded people when you crave stability.
You admire joyful people when you crave lightness.
You admire people who speak truth when you crave freedom.

Admiration is direction.
It is your inner self pointing toward who you are becoming.

A Story: The Young Man Who Modeled His Reinvention on a Stranger

Julian was twenty-eight, burnt out and unsure of his place in the world.
He worked a job he didn't love and spent most evenings feeling lost.

One night he heard a speaker at a community event.
The man was forty-five, confident, articulate, funny and unexpectedly kind.

Julian admired him instantly.

Not because he wanted the man's exact life, but because he wanted the qualities he radiated:

Calm.
Integrity.
Strength.
Presence.

Instead of shrugging off the admiration, Julian studied him.

He watched how he spoke, how he listened, how he carried himself.
He paid attention to the man's routines and values.
He read every book the man recommended.
He asked him thoughtful questions after events.
He didn't mimic him.
He learned from him.

Over time, Julian began to change.

He spoke more clearly.
He treated people with more intention.

His confidence grew.
His purpose sharpened.

He later said, "I stopped trying to copy him and started trying to become the version of myself that admired him."

That is the essence of this chapter.

Admiration Without Comparison

There is a difference between:

Comparison, which shrinks you.
and
Admiration, which expands you.

Comparison says, "They are better."
Admiration says, "They show me what's possible."

Comparison leads to shame.
Admiration leads to growth.

Reinvention requires choosing the second path.

Who You Admire Is a Map

Make a list of five people you admire.

They can be:

- Friends
- Teachers
- Artists
- Writers
- Public figures

• Creators
• Entrepreneurs
• Performers
• Athletes
• Activists
• Storytellers
• People in your community
• Anyone who makes you think, "There's something in them that feels like a missing piece of me"

Then ask:

• What qualities do they have that I want?
• What habits do they maintain that I avoid?
• What do they tolerate?
• What do they refuse to tolerate?
• How do they speak?
• How do they move through the world?
• What do they believe about themselves?
• What do they invest in?
• What do they avoid?
• What risks do they take?
• What boundaries do they hold?

You're not studying their life.
You're studying the qualities that resonate with your next identity.

What to Ask ChatGPT

Use AI as a coach while studying your admired people.

Try:

• "Help me analyze the qualities I admire in this person so I can build them into my life."
• "What habits would I need to adopt to reflect these qualities?"
• "Help me identify patterns in the people I admire."
• "Create a simple plan for me to embody these traits."

Admiration becomes a blueprint instead of a longing.

Your Action Step: Choose One Trait to Practice This Week

Pick one quality from someone you admire.
Just one.

Then ask:

"What is the smallest daily action that expresses this trait?"

Examples:

Admire someone's courage?
Say one brave sentence today.

Admire someone's calm?
Practice a two-minute breathing pause before reacting.

Admire someone's creativity?
Spend ten minutes making something.

Admire someone's clarity?
Edit one thought that creates confusion.

Admire someone's generosity?
Do one kind act.

Reinvention is built one trait at a time.
One decision at a time.
One modeled behavior at a time.

Admiration tells you where you are going.
Action gets you there.

Chapter 28. Host an "I'm Done" Ritual and Release the Old You

Reinvention is not only about building a new life.
It is equally about releasing the version of yourself who kept you small.

This chapter is a ceremony.
A turning point.
A declaration.

There is extraordinary power in saying, "I'm done."
Done carrying what was too heavy.
Done repeating what never worked.
Done performing identities assigned to you by others.
Done replaying old stories.
Done shrinking, apologizing, delaying or dimming.

Every reinvention needs a moment of release.
This chapter gives you that moment.

Why Ritual Matters in Reinvention

Humans have used ritual for thousands of years.
Not because rituals are dramatic, but because they anchor internal change.

A ritual:

- Marks a transition
- Creates emotional clarity
- Signals closure
- Prepares the mind for a new path
- Gives physical form to an inner decision

When you externalize a shift, it becomes real.

This chapter is your personal ceremony for letting go.

A Story: The Man Who Burned His Should-Have List

At forty-eight, Marcus carried two decades of regret.
The jobs he didn't apply for.
The trips he didn't take.
The boundaries he didn't set.
The marriage he stayed in too long.
The creative dreams he buried.

One night he wrote every "should have" and "I wish I had" on index cards.
Dozens of them.

He drove to a safe fire pit at a local park.
He burned them quietly, one by one.

Not out of anger.
Out of acknowledgment.

When the last card turned to ash, he felt an unexpected peace.

He said, "I didn't burn the past. I burned the permission it had to define me."

His reinvention did not begin with a plan.
It began with release.

How to Host Your "I'm Done" Ritual

This ritual is simple.
It is personal.
It is powerful.

Choose a setting:

- A backyard
- A balcony
- A quiet park
- A favorite room
- A journal
- A candle
- A bowl of water
- A fireproof container
- A tear-out page
- Anything that feels intentional

You don't need anything ceremonial.
Presence is the ceremony.

Then create two lists:

List 1: "What I'm Done Carrying"
Write everything you are done holding:

Old beliefs
Old relationships
Old fears
Old stories
Old patterns
Old expectations
Old shame
Old self-doubt

Old guilt
Old habits that dim you

List 2: "What I'm Choosing Instead"
Write the identity you are stepping into:

Clarity
Confidence
Creative power
Peace
Direction
Self-respect
Visibility
Joy
Boldness
Health
Freedom
Purpose
New patterns that lift you

Then choose a release method:

You can tear it
Burn it safely
Sink it in water
Fold it and store it out of sight
Read it aloud
Bury it
Shred it
Or simply close the journal on the old chapter

Do what feels true to your spirit.

Then say one sentence:

"I'm done with who I was. I'm choosing who I become next."

This is not symbolic.
It is psychological.
The brain responds to ritual as if it were a contract.

This chapter is your contract with yourself.

What to Ask ChatGPT

Use AI to help you craft your ritual.

Try:

- "Help me write a release list for my 'I'm done' ritual."
- "Help me write a declaration for the identity I'm choosing now."
- "Give me a ceremony script that matches my personality."
- "Help me clarify what I'm releasing and what I'm stepping into."

Ritual becomes powerful when your intention is clear.

Your Action Step: Host Your Ritual Within the Next 72 Hours

Don't put it off.
Don't wait for the perfect day.
Don't overthink it.

Choose a time.
Choose a space.
Choose your lists.
Release the old.
Claim the new.

Reinvention becomes real the moment you say:

"I'm done with what held me back. I'm ready for my next era."

This chapter is your doorway.

Walk through it.

Conclusion. Reinvention Begins the Moment You Decide Your Life Isn't Finished

Reinvention is not a dramatic event.
It is a decision.

A decision to stop living by momentum.
A decision to stop apologizing for wanting more.
A decision to stop shrinking into old versions of yourself.
A decision to stop letting the past dictate the possible.
A decision to choose consciousness over autopilot.
A decision to trust that your next era can be bigger, deeper, kinder and truer than what came before.

People believe reinvention requires bravery.
It doesn't.
It requires honesty.

Honesty about what you want.
Honesty about what you're tired of.
Honesty about who you are when no one's looking.
Honesty about the life you know you could live if you stopped delaying it.

Everything in this book has been leading you toward one truth:

You get to choose again.

You get to decide that your story is far from done.
You get to design a new identity.
You get to rebuild patterns that support the person you are becoming.
You get to release the identities that were handed to you.

You get to step into a version of yourself that your younger self would be proud of.

Reinvention is not a phase.
It is a practice.

You practice clarity.
You practice courage.
You practice boundaries.
You practice visibility.
You practice joy.
You practice new habits, new thoughts, new choices, new paths.
You practice being the future version of yourself until it becomes true.

And slowly, quietly, magnificently, you change.

Not because life forced you to.
Not because someone demanded it.
Not because you lost everything.

But because you finally realized:

"I deserve a life that fits me. I deserve a chance to begin again."

Reinvention is not the end of something.
It is the return to yourself.

You are not late.
You are right on time.
You are exactly where your next era begins.
And you already have everything you need.

All that's left is the choosing.

Your next chapter is waiting.

Choose it.

Reinvention Bot Toolkit

A practical set of tools, prompts and scripts designed to help you build the next version of yourself with clarity and support.

---

1. Identity Reset Prompts

These prompts help you clarify who you are becoming.

Ask the Reinvention Bot:

• "Help me describe the future version of myself in one paragraph."
• "List ten qualities of my next era self."
• "Show me the habits, routines and environments that match this identity."
• "Rewrite my old labels into new ones that support my future."

Use these when:
You feel lost, stuck or unsure about what your reinvention looks like.

---

2. Daily Reinvention Routines

Quick routines that support consistency.

Ask the Reinvention Bot:

• "Create a ten minute morning routine that aligns with my new identity."
• "Give me three daily non negotiables for the person I am becoming."
• "Write a simple evening reflection that keeps me on track."
• "Give me one tiny action each day that builds momentum."

Use these when:
You need structure without overwhelm.

---

3. Decision Making Clarity Tools

Support for choices large and small.

Ask the Reinvention Bot:

• "Help me choose between two paths based on my next identity."
• "Give me questions that help me make decisions with clarity."
• "Show me how each option aligns or misaligns with my future."

Use these when:
You feel pulled between old patterns and new possibilities.

---

4. Nervous Yes Support Scripts

Say yes to opportunities that stretch you.

Ask the Reinvention Bot:

• "Help me understand why this opportunity feels scary and why it might be worth doing."
• "Write a confidence script for stepping outside my comfort zone."
• "Give me five possible positive outcomes of saying yes."

Use these when:
You want courage, not pressure.

---

5. Boundary Building Tools

Helpful for protecting your energy and identity.

Ask the Reinvention Bot:

• "Help me write a calm, clear boundary for this situation."
• "Give me a script for saying no without guilt."
• "Help me express my limits with confidence."

Use these when:
You are outgrowing old expectations.

---

6. Old Story Rewrite Tools

Rewriting identity from the inside out.

Ask the Reinvention Bot:

• "Help me rewrite this limiting story into one that empowers me."
• "Give me two versions of a memory: the one I lived and the one I choose now."
• "Show me how this old belief has shaped my life and how to release it."

Use these when:
The past tries to pull you back.

---

7. Creativity and Curiosity Boosters

For sparking expansion and forward movement.

Ask the Reinvention Bot:

• "Give me ten creative sparks for my next era."
• "Help me explore something new that matches my reinvention."
• "List three small adventures I can take this week."

Use these when:
You want to feel alive again.

---

8. Environment and Energy Reset Tools

Support for spaces that match your new life.

Ask the Reinvention Bot:

• "Help me redesign one corner of my home to reflect my next identity."
• "Give me simple beauty upgrades that cost under twenty dollars."
• "Create a one week declutter plan based on emotional alignment."

Use these when:
Your space feels like it belongs to an older version of you.

---

9. Future Self Guidance Letters

Daily alignment with who you are becoming.

Ask the Reinvention Bot:

• "Write me a letter from my future self about the life I am building."
• "Give me encouragement from my future self on a hard day."
• "Describe what my life looks like in five years if I stay consistent."

Use these when:
You need inspiration driven by clarity rather than fantasy.

---

10. Reinvention Accountability Tools

For staying on track.

Ask the Reinvention Bot:

- "Give me a weekly check in to measure my progress."
- "List the patterns I am releasing and the ones I am adopting."
- "Help me track my reinvention without judgment."

Use these when:
You want gentle structure instead of pressure.

---

11. Drop the Old Life Checklist

A simple list for letting go.

Ask the Reinvention Bot:

- "Help me list what I am done carrying into my next chapter."
- "Give me a release statement for each item."
- "Help me prepare my 'I'm done' ritual."

Use these when:
You are ready to close a chapter with intention.

---

12. Signature Goal Blueprint

Turning a dream into a plan.

Ask the Reinvention Bot:

- "Help me choose one signature goal for my next era."
- "Break this goal into small steps based on my energy level."
- "Create a plan that balances ambition with self care."

Use these when:
You need direction that feels aligned instead of overwhelming.

---

13. Reinvention Recovery Tools

For days when life is heavy.

Ask the Reinvention Bot:

- "Help me restart my reinvention even after a setback."
- "Give me one compassionate step for today."
- "Show me how to rebuild momentum without pressure."

Use these when:
You feel discouraged, tired or off track.

---

14. Reinvention Vocabulary Builder

Language shapes identity.

Ask the Reinvention Bot:

- "Help me replace these old phrases with empowered ones."
- "Give me a list of words that match my next era self."
- "Rewrite my internal dialogue so it supports my growth."

Use these when:
Your thoughts need recalibration.

---

15. Reinvention Summary Tools

Create clarity after finishing the book.

Ask the Reinvention Bot:

- "Help me summarize the identity shifts I have made."
- "List my new habits, boundaries and intentions."
- "Give me a simple roadmap for my next ninety days."

Use these when:

You want to continue your reinvention with direction and strength.

About the Author

Sugar Gay Isber McMillan is a Texas artist, designer, educator and author of more than eighty books across art history, creativity, reinvention and modern technology. Her work blends storytelling, research and practical guidance, helping readers learn new skills, stay curious and use tools like ChatGPT to shape the next version of their lives.

Sugar has designed jewelry for films, television, museums and private collectors around the world. She is the Creative Ambassador for Fire Mountain Gems and hosts *Sugar and Her Bot* on Made It Myself TV, a series that teaches viewers how to work with AI as a supportive partner in creativity and problem solving. She also teaches jewelry design at Austin Community College.

Her writing spans multiple collections, including the Talk to Your Tools guides, the Learn While You Color series and memoir projects such as *Let Me Tell You About My Fabulous Life*. Each book is designed to offer clarity, creativity and accessible learning for readers at any stage of life.

Sugar holds a B.A. in Journalism, M.A.s in Humanities and Visual Arts and an advanced degree in Information Technology. She is certified in ChatGPT for Business Applications through Microsoft and also works as a technical writer for a global technology company.

Through The WOW Book Co., she continues to build a growing library of books that help people imagine, learn and reinvent themselves with confidence.

About the Reinvention Bot Book

Reinvention Bot is a practical guide for anyone ready to reset their life. Built on clear steps and daily actions, this book shows you how to release old patterns, build a stronger identity and use simple conversations with ChatGPT to support your next chapter. It offers structure, encouragement and tools you can use every day to stay focused on the person you are becoming.

Follow Sugar

Instagram: @SugarGayIsber
Amazon Author Page: amazon.com/author/sugargayisbermcmillan
Website: TheWOWBookCo.com
For media or collaborations: GayIsber@gmail.com